MEANS AND ENDS

THIS IS THE EIGHTH OF THE
WALTER NEURATH MEMORIAL LECTURES
WHICH ARE GIVEN ANNUALLY EACH SPRING ON
SUBJECTS REFLECTING THE INTERESTS OF
THE FOUNDER
OF THAMES AND HUDSON

THE DIRECTORS WISH TO EXPRESS
PARTICULAR GRATITUDE TO THE GOVERNORS AND
MASTER OF BIRKBECK COLLEGE
UNIVERSITY OF LONDON
FOR THEIR GRACIOUS SPONSORSHIP OF
THESE LECTURES

MEANS AND ENDS

REFLECTIONS
ON THE HISTORY OF
FRESCO PAINTING

E.H. GOMBRICH

THAMES AND HUDSON
LONDON

I gratefully accepted the Master's invitation to give the Walter Neurath Memorial Lecture, as my memories of Walter Neurath surely go back further than those of most people in this hall. Forty-one years ago Walter Neurath commissioned me to write my first book. The story is sufficiently characteristic of that extraordinary publisher to tell it on this occasion. He was at that time editing a series of books for a Viennese publishing house called Steyrermühl under the title Wissenschaft für Kinder *(Knowledge for Children). Somebody had suggested an English* History of the World *for inclusion in this series, and he asked me whether I could shorten and translate it in a hurry. Having read a few pages of terribly patronizing stuff I told him I did not like the book and added with the recklessness of total inexperience that I'd rather write such a book myself. Walter Neurath took me at my word and asked me to submit a trial chapter. I did so, but by the time he had read it and offered me a contract only six weeks remained till he wanted the manuscript. Don't ask me how I met this deadline; all I can say is that I have slowed down considerably since. Walter Neurath never slowed down. The titles, the series, the authors he launched in the course of a life which was prematurely cut short are astounding; and, as you know, his work is being continued by his family who are happily with us.*

My CHOICE OF SUBJECT today is proof enough that I have indeed slowed down. I shall present some second thoughts about an idea I put forward sixteen years ago in my book *Art and Illusion*:[1] I mean the idea, which is more familiar in the theory of architecture than in the criticism of painting, that form follows function or that the end determines the means. Of course slogans of this kind can never have more than what is called a heuristic value: they draw attention to the kind of question the historian should ask in confronting the monuments of the past. Admittedly, no human action and no human creation is likely to serve only one end; we often find a whole hierarchy of ends and of means; but we can also discern a dominant purpose without which the event would not have happened at all. Moreover, in human affairs means can easily become ends: as is indicated in the formula 'Art for Art's sake'. In trying to illustrate some aspects of this complex interaction by looking at the history of fresco painting, I must ask for indulgence on several scores. First, I shall be concerned with means, but shall not be pedantic about media. I have juxtaposed two famous murals, both painted in the last decade of the Quattrocento, Ghirlandaio's frescoes in S. Maria Novella in Florence and Leonardo's *Last Supper* in S. Maria delle Grazie in Milan. I shall not enter into the question of the experimental technique allegedly used by Leonardo to avoid the need for rapidity connected with fresco painting; in fact I shall use the term 'fresco' in a Pickwickian sense to stand for any mural or indeed ceiling painting of an interior. That I shall have to be ruthlessly selective in my examples culled from a few millennia goes without saying. What may need saying is that, here as later, I shall often use familiar rather than unfamiliar landmarks without, alas, being able to dwell on them as they deserve. They serve here as evidence to support a theoretical thesis concerning Means and Ends, in the history not of art but of image-making.

< 1 Domenico Ghirlandaio. *Life of St John the Baptist*, 1490. S. Maria Novella, Florence

2 Leonardo. *Last Supper*, c. 1495. S. Maria delle Grazie, Milan

The end or dominant purpose of the two frescoes happens to be reasonably clear. The story of Ghirlandaio's cycle, as told by Vasari, was a favourite example of Aby Warburg's which served him to break down the purely aesthetic approach of nineteenth-century art historians.[2] It was painted in the choir of one of the great preaching churches of Florence, of which the patronage belonged to the banker Francesco Sassetti, an associate of the Medici firm, who naturally wanted it decorated – if that is the word – with frescoes telling the story of his name saint, St Francis. Alas, S. Maria Novella is a Dominican not a Franciscan church, and the suggestion was too much for the monks. In the end Sassetti withdrew to S. Trinità and ceded his rights at S. Maria Novella to another banker of the Medici circle whose Christian name was luckily Giovanni, Giovanni Tornabuoni. No objections were raised to the life of St John the Baptist being painted in the Dominican church. The main purpose of the other example, the *Last Supper* in the monastery of S. Maria delle Grazie in Milan is almost self-evident. It was the tradition to represent the Last Supper on the walls of refectories, and in this respect Leonardo conformed to usage, though his conception of the scene was less traditional.

My purpose in showing these examples, however, is not only to recall the social fabric in which image-making was embedded in Renaissance Italy, but to illustrate my text for these reflections on Ends and Means. It is an important text, for it comes from Leonardo da Vinci's *Treatise on Painting*, a compilation of the master's thoughts made by his pupil Melzi. It roundly attacks such frescoes as Ghirlandaio's in the Tornabuoni Chapel:

Why the arrangement of figures one on top of the other should be avoided.

There is a universal custom followed by those who paint on the walls of chapels which is much to be deplored. They depict one scene with its landscape and buildings on one level, then they go up and make another, varying the point of sight, and then on to the third and to the fourth in such a way that one wall is seen to be made with four points of sight, which is the height of stupidity on the part of these masters. We know that the point of sight must correspond to the eye-level of the beholder of the scene.[3]

The principle which is laid down by Leonardo, and which he followed in Milan, may be formulated as 'one wall, one space, one scene'. It may remind the literary historian of the three unities demanded by Aristotle for the tragedy – those of time, of place, and of action. And like the Aristotelian critics, dismissing Shakespeare for his disregard of this principle, Leonardo is scathing about his colleagues who violate his unities, saying in another note that a painting with various horizons looks like a shop with merchandise displayed in various rectangular pigeonholes.[4]

You may be sorry to hear about Leonardo's prejudice, which led him thus to ridicule some of the greatest creations of Italian painting, such as Piero della Francesca's cycle in the choir of S. Francesco in Arezzo; but I would plead so much at least in his favour that the practice of art historians and art publishers has come round to his point of view. We are usually shown these paintings in isolation, on the principle of one picture, one space, one scene; indeed in compiling this lecture it has come home to me how rare it is that frescoes are in fact shown in their setting, as they luckily are in Eve Borsook's book *Mural Painters of Tuscany*.[5]

But though isolation may serve the ends of the art historian and of the modern art lover, the painter of a fresco cycle had to contend with different demands, and Leonardo knew it. For his note continues:

If you ask me: how shall I paint on one wall the life of a saint which is divided into many incidents? My answer is that you must place the first plane at the eye-level of the beholder of the scene and on that plane represent the first scene in large size, and then diminishing the figures and buildings on the various hills and plains, as you go on, make the setting for the whole story. And as to the remainder of the wall, fill it with large trees in relation to the figures, or with angels, if they fit the story, or perhaps birds or clouds. If you do otherwise you will exert yourself in vain and all your work will go awry.[6]

Thus, the only concession which Leonardo was ready to make to the demands of the patron who wanted to have the whole life of his patron saint was to have one wall, one space, but several subsidiary scenes in that space: a vague analogy, if you like, to the eyewitness or

messenger report in a unified drama. We can illustrate the kind of compromise he had in mind from the Quattrocento frescoes in the Sistine Chapel, in Rome, but only approximately so, because they are high up on the wall and have many compartments. Botticelli, for instance, represented seven episodes of the story of Moses in one unified landscape, with the meeting of Moses and Jethro's daughters at the well in the centre, the fiery bush in the background, and the Exodus squeezed into the corner – a compromise which makes one wonder whether the game of unity is worth the candle.

Not surprisingly, the most consistent application of Leonardo's demands was attempted by his pupil Bernardino Luini in the colossal fresco of *Golgotha* in S. Maria degli Angioli in Lugano. This, too, is not on eye-level, and the relegation of the story of the Passion to a kind of background stage reminds us that there really was no future in this kind of compromise.

Why, then, did Leonardo go out of his way to recommend such an awkward expedient? Clearly because, for him, painting had one overriding aim, on which he insisted in countless notes:

The elements of painted scenes must move those who look at them to experience the same emotions as those represented in the story, that is to feel terror, fear, fright or pain, grief and lamentation or pleasure, happiness and laughter . . . if they fail to do this the skill of the painter will have been in vain.[7]

We have a term for this effect, which Leonardo considers the true purpose of the painter's skill; we call it empathy. In confronting his *Last Supper* we should be troubled with the Apostles, defiant with Judas, and resigned with Christ, who has just announced His impending betrayal and passion. It almost goes without saying that this experience also demands a special kind of looking. We must *concentrate*, as the wisdom of language has it, and we must focus on each of the figures in turn as we immerse ourselves in the event depicted. It is towards this end that all the painter's means must be mobilized. In order fully to appreciate the psychological relationship of the figures, we must be made also to sense the space in which they move and act.

13

< 3 Sandro Botticelli. *The Meeting of Moses and Jethro's Daughters*, 1481–82. Sistine Chapel, Vatican

4 Bernardino Luini.
Golgotha, 1529–30.
S. Maria degli
Angioli, Lugano

Vasari in his description of the work notoriously singles out for praise the convincing accuracy of the fabric of the tablecloth; and even this minor detail must be understood as a visual aid, enhancing the im, mediacy of the beholder's experience that he is made to witness the momentous occasion of the Institution of the Eucharist. Unhappily we have no better word for this feeling than the omnibus term 'illusion', though of course nobody can be under a genuine illusion that he is confronted with a frozen event. The word we would need would have to correspond to the term 'fiction' in literature. Fiction can be vivid and convincing in evoking an imaginary event without anyone taking it to describe a real happening. I shall argue that in art and in literature this response depends on an inner coherence, a situational consistency. It was this coherence that Aristotle wanted to secure by his unities and Leonardo by his insistence on a consistent spatial setting. The idea of a succession of scenes showing the sky and then the floor on top of it was the height of stupidity (*somma stoltitia*), because it lacked this elementary situational coherence.

This is the point at which I have to hark back to a chapter of my book *Art and Illusion*, called 'Reflections on the Greek Revolution': not to recant the hypothesis I there presented, but to articulate it a little more. What I argued was that we put the cart before the horse if we follow the authors of classical antiquity in recounting the growth of *mimesis*, the imitation of nature, as a merely formal development. The development can only be understood as a means to a new end, namely the visual evocation of a mythical event. In ancient Greece the myths were not only recited in immutable sacred accounts; they were freely embroidered by poets and put on the stage so that the audience could experience the fear and pity that Aristotle considered the aim of tragedy. To do so the playwright had to be given licence to imagine the event as it might have happened, as a full-blooded interpretation of a human situation with which we can empathize. Hence the unities. I believe it was this same dominant aim, of showing not only the 'what' but the 'how' of an event, which also led Greek art to the observation of natural appearances, the rendering of expression, of anatomy, of space and of light. Form followed function. Whether or not, say, the ancient

5 Tomb of Sennedjem. Thebes, Egypt, xixth Dynasty

Egyptians could have mastered these skills seems to me irrelevant, because they used the image for a different purpose. With which we are back at Leonardo's problem. The images in ancient Egyptian tombs are certainly arranged in registers, but their function is predominantly symbolic, almost pictographic, ranging from the hieroglyphic inscription to the enumeration of activities serving the dead and the trials awaiting the dead in the after-life. Such images must be read sequentially, more or less as we read a text, and for this process a division into registers is an almost indispensable help.

We have no Greek murals from the decisive period, but paintings on vases appear to confirm that the emancipation from episodic narrative in zones went hand-in-hand with the new psychological

6 Kleitias. François Vase, *c.* 570 BC

7 The Brygos Painter. *Priam and Achilles*, skyphos, 5th c. BC

emphasis: contrast the François vase of the sixth century, with its many incidents, and the fifth-century *skyphos* by Brygos showing the Homeric episode of Priam asking Achilles for Hector's body, where our eyes must surely linger on the actions and gestures of the participants in this moving scene.

It seems that the painter Polygnotus, who was a contemporary of the great Greek tragedians of the fifth century, achieved the same psychological empathy, but was as yet unable to unify his scenes as completely.[8] So at least we are led to conclude by the description of his two murals at Delphi that we find in the ancient tourist guide by Pausanias.[9] Their subjects were episodes from the destruction of Troy and from Ulysses' descent to the Underworld, and it appears that he adapted something like the compromise suggested by Leonardo, distributing his figures and groups loosely over a steep ground so that those further back were shown higher up on the wall, as is indicated in Goethe's diagrammatic reconstruction.[10] There is a famous Greek vase (of

8 After J. W. von Goethe. *Polygnotus' Paintings in the Lesche at Delphi*, diagram, 1803

stone Sisyphus rock unnamed	vessel Tantalus bearers water	} toilers in vain	Penthesileia Paris Sarpedon Memnon Hector	} Trojans
Pero Nomia Callisto }				
	Meleager Ajax Thersites Palamedes Ajax	} Greeks, enemies of Ulysses		
Autonoë Actaeon Maira Iaseus Phocus } lovers	Patroclus Achilles Protesilaus Agamemnon Antilochus	} Greeks, friends of Ulysses	Olympus Marsyas Thamyris Pelias Schedius Promedon Orpheus	} teachers disciples poets patrons

19

9 The Niobid Painter. *Herakles and Athena*, calyx-krater, *c.* 455–450 BC

which the subject has been variously interpreted) which is generally believed to reflect the method of composition used by Polygnotus.

We do have a mural from a later period, the so-called Odyssey landscapes from the Esquiline in Rome, of the first century BC, which look like a perfect illustration of my hypothesis.[11] The demand that the artist allow us to visualize the 'how', rather than merely tell us 'what' happened, has led by now to the creation of scenes bathed in light and atmosphere, which we witness from afar; and yet the Greeks and Laestrygonians are individuals realized with the deft skill of a great tradition.

Precisely because the means had been found to this end, a new problem had arisen in adapting this type of composition to the needs of a mural. To appreciate this new problem, we need only pause for a moment to consider what happens when we enter a room or any other environment. We first look around to see where we are; we notice the wall; we inspect a detail; all these, and many other varieties of perception, require different ways of scanning and of focusing. For the visual evocation of a dramatic painting to come to life, you remember, we must focus on it mentally and scan it in a controlled way so as to interpret its coherence. What has been called by F. C. Bartlett 'the effort after meaning' makes us see the blue patch as water and the bright zone as a gap between the rocks. This may not take long, but it takes a measurable time. To perceive an interior also takes a moment, but here we look around in a sequence of roving eye-movements which soon completes our orientation. Now the decoration of a room, whether architectural or pictorial, need not slow down this alternative effort after meaning. On the contrary, by articulating the walls and the ceiling, the decoration may set accents for rapid scanning. We do not have to inspect every real or fictitious column or pilaster, because we quickly pick up correspondences and redundancies so that we can take the individual element as read. Note that to do so we also operate with an assumption of an expected coherence which enables us to accept whatever fiction the decorator may have introduced. He might for instance ask us to imagine that we look out of the room at various vistas, and he might use for this purpose the very means

10 *Ulysses Arriving in the Land of the Laestrygonians; The Laestrygonians*

of so-called illusionism which were developed, if I am right, for
the alternative purpose of dramatic evocation in paintings and prob-
ably also on the stage. Now, the Odyssey landscapes were originally
part of a decorative scheme suggesting a series of openings through
which we look at various episodes from the epic; it is clear that here
the two tests of coherence come into conflict – it is a curious room
that appears to open on various different episodes separated in time
and in place.

In abstract terms there are two ways out of this artistic dilemma. The
painter can turn the whole wall into the semblance of one scene, in

Attacking the Ships, 1st c. BC. From a house on the Esquiline, Rome

fact he can make the whole room a fictional setting of an imagined event. This is what the master of the Villa dei Misteri near Pompeii (ill. 11) has done. He has created a shallow stage between us and the fictitious as distinct from the real wall, enlarging his figures to a scale which is easily taken in and which has an enormous dramatic impact, even though we are not quite sure what ritual is being performed. Alternatively the artist can save the coherence of his fiction by introducing the time-honoured device of a tale within a tale. Translated into visual terms, this means a representation within a representation. The decorators of Rome and Pompeii were past masters in ringing the changes on this sophisticated device: individual framed pictures, to be inspected by controlled scanning, are presented as part of the whole fictitious interior which may open out into vistas (ill. 12). Whether or not the Romans used the laws of perspective for these vistas is still an open question. I think it matters less than the way they coped with the principle of coherence. Vitruvius, in the Age of Augustus, notoriously took the principle quite literally, insisting that in illusionistic murals the painter must keep strictly to forms which are architecturally viable

11 *The Initiation of Brides into the Dionysiac Mysteries,*

and would stand up in reality. Playful and grotesque fictitious struc/
tures he rejected outright, without perceiving that their very flimsiness
and their visual paradoxes enhanced their character as decorative
fiction.[12] Be that as it may, the words in which this canonical authority
condemned the painting of impossible situations had an enormous
influence on the history of criticism,[13] and may even have been at the
back of Leonardo's mind when he attacked the mural painters of his
time for their inconsistencies.

1st c. BC. Villa dei Misteri, Pompeii

12 Mural decoration,
1st c. AD.
Casa dei Vettii,
Pompeii

Soon the mural painter was to contend with a much more weighty kind of opposition, which was indeed to change the course of art. Christians could not ignore the Second Commandment, which enjoins them not to make 'any graven image, or any likeness of anything that is in heaven above, or that is in the earth beneath, or that is in the water under the earth' (Exodus 20:4). In the light of this text, the miracle is really that, unlike Judaism and most of Islam, the Christian Church in the West continued to tolerate the making of images in religious contexts. The concession which made this possible is best formulated in the pronouncement of Pope Gregory the Great which acknowledges the didactic purpose of images: painting is, to those who cannot read, what letters are to those who can. To simplify but not, I hope, to falsify an immensely complex issue, we might say that this restriction of the function of religious art redirected the image-makers towards the exploration of those pictographic methods which had never been entirely extinct.

13 *Adoration of the Magi*, 4th c. AD. Cubicle of SS. Pietro e Marcellino, Rome

14 *Old Testament Scenes*, 4th c. AD. Catacomb of Vigna Magna, Rome

The murals in the Roman catacombs illustrate to perfection the difference between such a pictograph and what I have called dramatic evocation. In SS. Pietro e Marcellino, we recognize at the back the Adoration of the Magi, flanked by Moses striking the rock and Noah emerging from the Ark. It is a suitable example because nobody can have thought that the Ark, which was, after all, made to accom-modate a pair of every species, can have been smaller than Noah himself. It is a pictograph in the sense that the image of a floating box marks the figure as Noah, and that the figure generates scarcely more fictitious space around it than do the decorative scrolls. Once the image has thus been reduced to a sign, Leonardo's problem of inconsistent spaces disappears by itself.

In the murals from Vigna Magna you can read off a large number of examples of divine intervention arranged in various registers: above, Moses striking the rock, the miracle of the loaves and fishes, the Adora-tion of the Magi, the figure of an *orans*, and the hieroglyph of Noah once more; below, Daniel in the lions' den, Tobit with his fish, the healing of the lame man who walks off with his bed, the raising of Lazarus, and poor Lazarus at the gate of Dives. Clearly what mattered here is the *what*, not the *how*, of the event. Think of what a contemporary of the Laocoön group would have made of the scene of Daniel in the lions' den!

We know that the practice, censured by Leonardo, of telling a story sequentially in various registers was exemplified in the principal church of Christendom, in the original Basilica of St Peter's, where there was a mural cycle of which we have at least a copy, made before the church was finally pulled down to make way for the present structure.[14] The exact date and state of this immensely influential cycle cannot be established with certainty; suffice it to say that here we again see what I have called the pictographic method. This is exemplified in the pic- ture of Noah's Ark, fairly early in a long cycle which has to be read sequentially for its inner coherence to emerge.

We usually associate Early Christian wall decoration with mosaics rather than with mural paintings. The durability of the medium has a lot to do with this, but there are other reasons more closely connected

15 Jacopo Grimaldi. *Mural Decoration of Old St Peter's, Rome*, drawing, 1620

16 *Adoration of the Magi*, mosaic, *c.* AD 435. S. Maria Maggiore, Rome

with the shift in the role of the image. Realistic painting is wedded to
the observation of nature in all its variety. The pictograph stands in no
need of such servitude. Just as the scribe is free to pen the sacred word
in letters of gold on a purple page, to express his veneration and awe,
so the designer of a pictographic narrative is free to enhance his message with all the resources of visual splendour. What he loses in terms
of focused vision is amply made up by the gain for the roving eye.
Whether or not those who could not read were able to take in the exact
meaning of some of the figures on the mosaic of the triumphal arch
of S. Maria Maggiore, which still baffle the scholars,[15] may be a
moot point, but that laity and clergy alike would feel the import of
so much gold and solemnity we cannot doubt. As a result, the mural
in the Middle Ages became something like a poor relation of the
more splendid media such as the mosaic and the stained-glass window.

It was said of the lectures of a Harvard Professor of Art History, 'drop your pencil and you have missed a century'. My case is worse; I shall have to drop a handful of centuries in selecting just one of the better preserved examples of a medieval mural – the apse of the Catalan church of S. María de Tahull, in which we see the Virgin enthroned, approached by the three Magi, marked with their names.[16] In the vault we see the figure of Abel with his sacrifice accepted; no doubt there was the corresponding image of the rejection of Cain on the other side. In the apex there is the symbol of the Lamb of God, and beneath a row of Prophets there are fabulous animals which may be purely decorative. What such a Romanesque ensemble confirms is what I have been leading up to. There is no visual distinction in this style between the symbolic, the narrative and the decorative. What we call the Adoration of the Magi is really the Epiphany, the first homage by the mighty rulers to the incarnate Word. It is no more the visualization of an earthly reality than is the Lamb of God in the centre. Nothing in his didactic and ritualistic purpose impeded the artist from making full use of the framework provided for him by the architect. The articulations of the building coincide with the grouping of the images.

When did this grand and consistent use of images disintegrate, and what were the pressures which led to that revival of the classical conception we call the Renaissance? It is a question which has engaged the minds of historians for generations, and you will not expect me to produce a clear-cut answer. All I want to do is to draw your attention to one element in the story which seems to me to parallel the development in classical antiquity. I mean the increasing demand for what I have called dramatic evocation, the return to the desire not to be told only what happened according to the Scriptures but how it happened, what events must have looked like to an eyewitness.

I agree with those who connect this decisive change with the new role of the popular preacher in the thirteenth century. It was the friars who took the Gospel story to the people and spared no effort to make the faithful re-live and re-enact it in their minds. It is well known that St Francis celebrated Christmas at Greccio in this way, actually bringing an ox and an ass into the church, and maybe also a live baby.

17 *Virgin and Child Enthroned, Adored by the Magi*, AD 1123. From S. María de Tahull >

It was in the Franciscan tradition also that there grew up that important technique of devotion which involves this kind of imaginative identi/ fication. That great historian of Christian iconography, Emile Mâle, stressed the crucial importance in this context of the *Meditations on the Life of Christ* by the Pseudo/Bonaventura, and of the miracle plays.[17] He has been accused of overstatement, and no doubt there were other factors, but I still think that he had the right intuition, and that the change of attitude to the sacred narrative engendered by the new conception of teaching and preaching cannot be left out of the history of art.

Let me here quote in evidence the description of the arrival of the Magi from Nicholas Love's English translation of the *Meditations on the Life of Christ*, made before 1400, which I have only slightly modernized:

And so imagine we and set we our mind and our thought as we were present in the place where this was done at Bethlehem, beholding how these three Kings comen with gret multitude . . . and how they alight down of the dromedars they had ridden upon, before that simple house and manner of stable in which our Lord Jesus was born. And then, our Lady hearing great noise and stirring of people, anon took her sweet child into her armes, and they come into that house, and soon as they see the child they kneel adown and reverently and devoutly honoured him as a king. . . . Now we take good heed, as to the manner of speaking of both parties, how our lady, with a manner of honest shamefastness, holding down her eyes toward the earth, speaketh and answereth sadly and shortly to their askings, for she has no liking to speak much . . .[18]

I need not elaborate on the clash between this account and the Romanesque fresco from Spain (ill. 17).

I think it could be argued that, at first, sculpture was more pliable to these new demands than painting was. The rendering of the indi/ vidual figure, as it responded to any situation, achieved a dramatic intensity with Nicola and Giovanni Pisano which has never been sur/ passed. But once these protagonists were felt to be in need of a con/ vincing stage, a consistent spatial setting, only painting could provide all the means to this end. It is at this point of the story that I would

18 Nicola Pisano. *Adoration of the Magi*, relief, 1265–68. Siena Cathedral

place the figure of Giotto. He was the narrative genius who knew how to transform the traditional pictograph into a living presence, and the participants into beings with an inner life of inexhaustible intensity.

Thus my interpretation of the growth of representational mastery relies on the same basic principle that I have postulated for the develop-ment of illusionism in ancient art. It would indeed be possible to take up the story of Renaissance art from here and chronicle the progress towards this goal, in which of course the conquest of perspective and of anatomy play their part.[19] Leonardo's preparations for his *Adoration of the Magi* illustrate these increasing concerns, which bring in the resources of science and justify the role in the history of this develop-ment which historians have assigned to him since the days of Vasari.

35

19-21 Giotto. *Adoration of the Magi*; detail; section of south wall, *c.* 1306. Arena Chapel, Padua

22 Leonardo. Study for *Adoration of the Magi*, c. 1480

23 Leonardo. Figure studies, c. 1480

These sketches were made by Leonardo not for a fresco but for an altarpiece – another area where the new aim of painting might clash with the traditional function of the visual image in the Christian Church.[20] Suffice it to say that, in a sense, Vasari's story would have to be supplemented and perhaps adjusted to describe the various means by which artists tried to extricate themselves from these conflicts of ends.

In the story of fresco painting Giotto stands at the beginning of a long and complex series of problem solutions. Remember that, in the tradition he inherited, the symbolic, narrative and decorative elements could peacefully coexist within any fresco cycle; it is a coexistence which was inevitably threatened by the new demand for convincing evocation of significant events. As if to acknowledge this new need for differentiation, Giotto introduced a visual distinction between symbolism and narration: the didactic images of the Virtues and Vices are distributed below in grisaille, suggesting fictitious statuary rather than living flesh, while the stories above are told with all the resources of his new realism. In thus introducing the device which the Swedish art historian Sven Sandström, in a thoughtful book, has called *Levels of Unreality*,[21] Giotto assigned a special status to those personifications which in the tradition of Western thought occupy a kind of no-man's-land between spiritual entities and mere abstractions. But the demands of a full narrative did not allow him at the same time to escape that stacked arrangement which Leonardo described as the height of stupidity – for this effect was inseparable from his achievement. As long as narrative was conceived as a writing on the wall, concentrating on the 'what' rather than the 'how', there was no visual jump between the scenes; but when we are asked to focus on the single frame which Alberti was to liken to a window opening on to a scene, the multiple vistas carry within them the seeds of their own destruction. This is so even before the introduction of perspective makes the contradiction fully apparent.[22]

Art historians need no reminding that, in the early history of perspective, means and ends were sometimes out of phase. The first application of the new skill to fresco painting of which we know is

25 Domenico di Bartolo. *Activities of a Hospital*, 1441–44. West wall of Pellegrinaio, Ospedale della Scala, Siena

Masaccio's majestic *Trinity* from S. Maria Novella, in Florence; but what it represents within this highly convincing fictitious chapel is not an imagined reality but a purely symbolic image, a reminder of a doctrine which cannot be visualized at all. The real presence in art of the First Person of the Trinity in so tangible a form is not easy to reconcile with the Decalogue, but it does not seem to have disturbed Masaccio's contemporaries.

In the Brancacci Chapel of S. Maria del Carmine in Florence, of course Masaccio made use of the compartmentalized scheme; and so did any number of masters of the Quattrocento. But there are signs that in the course of the century the method began to look old-fashioned. Mantegna had used the traditional scheme in the Ovetari Chapel in the Church of the Eremitani, Padua, but in the Camera degli Sposi in the Castello in Mantua he created an interior of astounding originality,

41

< 24 Masaccio. *The Trinity*, 1425. S. Maria Novella, Florence

26 Andrea Mantegna. Camera degli Sposi, *c.* 1464–74. Palazzo Ducale, Mantua >

applying the basic devices of the mural painters of antiquity in an entirely novel fashion – note the fictitious vistas and the famous open roundel in the ceiling through which people appear to look down into the room, and note the family group over the mantelpiece which confronts us almost bodily in the narrow zone before the fictitious wall or curtain. But in this extraordinary room Mantegna did not have to contend with the narrative aims of Christian didactic art, which proved so hard to assimilate to the novel means of illusionistic painting. Where a sequence of scenes was demanded, the easiest way out of the dilemma was still provided by the real architectural articulation of a wall, the division into lunettes each of which could accommodate a scene with its own space, as with Domenico di Bartolo's room in the Ospedale della Scala in Siena. There is only a small step from this familiar scheme to Pinturicchio's solution, which completely con-forms to Leonardo's demand for the unities of wall, space and scene – I am referring to the beautiful interior of a chapel in S. Maria Mag-giore at Spello. There are three scenes on three walls: the Annuncia-

27, 28 Pinturicchio. *Annunciation;*

tion, the Nativity, and Christ among the Doctors. The artist did not find it all that easy to fill these walls with significant detail, but the general impression of these spacious scenes is much more pleasing than isolated illustrations might suggest. The chapel was completed in 1501, and we may regard it as a landmark. For in the sixteenth century the old compartmentalized system was no longer acceptable. Others must have shared Leonardo's view.

There is one work, of course, which evades the problem and wholly defies categorization. I refer to Michelangelo's Sistine ceiling in which the individual stories or scenes are not stacked on top of each other, precisely because they are in an unreal sphere on top of a fictitious architecture. Whether Leonardo would have approved of this inven⁄tion or regarded it as a dodge we shall never know. He would hardly have objected to Raphael's Stanze in the Vatican, which have become the standard example of the classic solution of fresco decoration with the lunettes in each of the vaulted rooms corresponding to one space and one topic, if not to one scene. Leonardo would have had no reason and

Christ among the Doctors, 1501. S. Maria Maggiore, Spello

29 Michelangelo. Vault of Sistine Chapel, 1508–12. Vatican

no right to object to the fact that these scenes do not start on floor level but above the dado. He had done the same in S. Maria delle Grazie; and indeed this is a practical precaution without which paintings on a wall soon succumb to the friction of crowds rubbing against them or fingering them.[23]

The base in the Stanza della Segnatura is not original, except for the fictitious reliefs under the *Parnassus*, which indicate that Raphael resorted to those 'degrees of unreality' we remember from Giotto. The idea was used with conviction in the next stanza, the Stanza dell' Eliodoro, where fictitious caryatids carry a kind of balustrade across which we look into the dramatic scenes which are, by themselves, far from simple. Indeed, if we analyse these first two Stanze, we may come

46

30 Raphael. Stanza della Segnatura, 1509–11. Vatican

31 Raphael. Stanza dell'Eliodoro, 1511–14. Vatican >

to reflect that their harmonious appearance is partly a matter of luck – ours as well as Raphael's. His first commissions in Rome involved the decoration of relatively small rooms, which almost asked for this harmonious solution. It was different with the Sala di Costantino, for here much larger walls demanded to be organized without resorting to that subdivision into registers which had become old-fashioned and unusable. Hence Raphael had to resort to the device of the tale within a tale. His dramatic scenes from the life of Constantine are represented as if they were woven hangings, suspended between niches with portraits of Popes, flanked by personifications who appear to be very much of our world of flesh, a strange reversal of Giotto's solution.

The variety of solutions of this problem of decoration, particularly among the pupils and followers of Raphael and other masters active in Rome, has recently been surveyed in a stimulating book by Catherine Dumont.[24] I wish I could turn its pages with you to introduce you to the many variations played on themes introduced by Raphael and Michelangelo and carried to extremes by the next generation – such as the crowded walls of the Sala Regia designed by Pierino del Vaga in

32 Raphael and Giulio Romano. Sala di Costantino, c. 1520–24. Vatican

33 Pierino del Vaga. Sala Regia, *c.* 1542–48. Castel S. Angelo, Rome

the Castel Sant'Angelo in Rome, which shows us layer upon layer of fictitious fictions. You will rightly be reminded here of the ancient examples I showed before, but Pompeii was of course undiscovered at that time. No doubt hints could be derived from some fragments of ancient painting found elsewhere, but what interests me is rather the reason why they were studied with such eagerness. I would suggest that they can be interpreted as the response to an inevitable conflict between ends and means which arises from the fact that decoration, sequential narrative and dramatic evocation each demand a different way of looking. If it was consistent with logic for Alberti to suggest that a painting representing an *istoria* should be conceived as a window through which we look at the scene, it followed that a frescoed wall should be similarly treated as a fictitious opening, as Peruzzi had done on Vitruvian principles in the Villa Farnesina, without, however,

49

34 Baldassare Peruzzi. Sala delle Prospettive, *c.* 1516. Villa Farnesina, Rome >

35 Giulio Romano. Sala dei Giganti, 1532–35. Palazzo del Te, Mantua

denying himself the privilege of introducing a fictitious frieze with
Ovidian scenes above the opening and various fictitious reliefs and
statues. But, in any case, why should the fiction of the opening be
restricted to the separate walls? Taken to its logical extreme the principle must in fact deny not only the wall but the room itself, which is
what Giulio Romano did in his Sala dei Giganti in Mantua – a
sensational showpiece which is not perhaps, the height of stupidity, but
the height of folly, when regarded as a room – precisely because it is the
ultimate in dramatic evocation, the equivalent of a 3-D horror film.

In the history of art these various forms of organized confusion are
generally discussed under the stylistic heading of Mannerism. When
I was a young student of the subject, Mannerism was supposed to

36 Giorgio Vasari. Sala dei Cento Giorni, 1546. Palazzo della Cancelleria, Rome

thrive on deliberate tensions, dilemmas and paradoxes. It seems to me
now that these dilemmas were not so much contrived as real: they were
the result of the means of illusion outrunning the ends of decoration
and of evocation, and creating problems for the artist which made a
harmonious solution extremely difficult if not impossible. The rich-
ness, and indeed the visual wit, of some of these decorative schemes is
not in doubt, but the imbalance between ends and means is unresolved,
whether we look at Vasari's Sala dei Cento Giorni, in the Cancelleria
in Rome, with its fictitious steps leading to fictitious scenes, or at
Francesco Salviati's Palazzo Sacchetti, with its panels uncomfortably
superimposed on fictitious columns. I believe we cannot do justice
to these complexities unless we supplement the purely formal and

53

37 Francesco Salviati. Sala Grande, 1553–54. Palazzo Sacchetti, Rome >

stylistic approach by the reconstruction of the problems facing the artist in the adjustment of means to ends and ends to means.[25]

I am emboldened to suggest this methodological rule because it may also help us in our appreciation of the next development in the history of fresco painting, the rise and proliferation of the so-called illusion- istic ceiling, which we associate with the style of the Baroque, though we know it to have been started early in the sixteenth century (notably with Correggio's cupolas, derived, perhaps, from Mantegna's vault). [26] I hope I shall not be accused of overplaying my hand if I suggest that this device can also be seen as a response to the dilemma which engaged our attention. For if there is one area in a large room to which Leonardo's unities can be applied without subterfuges and qualifica- tions, it is the ceiling. Imagine it as a fictional pane, and you look straight into heaven. The example shows in a particularly striking way how means will tend to generate ends. What looks like another purely formal or decorative device has the profoundest consequence on the resources of the image. It enabled the artist to recapture that unity of the symbolic, the narrative and the decorative, inherent in medieval art, which had disintegrated through those demands of dramatic evocation we have been concerned with. In heaven there is no distinction we can grasp between angels and those spiritual entities we call personifications.[27] Looking into heaven is in any case a vision- ary experience, where metaphors gain reality not as tangible repre- sentations but as meaning. The light of heaven is not earthly light but divine radiance, which is seen in the famous ceiling of S. Ignazio to shine on the heart of the saint, whence it is reflected into all parts of the globe. To call such a composition, with all its attendant symbolic beings and signs, illusionistic seems to me again to be straining the meaning of the word; but we may call it an evocation which turns us into visionary eyewitnesses of that mystery which the Church desires to convey to the faithful. No doubt the possibility of transforming the ceiling into a unified vision also attracted the secular rulers, with their desire for apotheoses and mythological eulogies; but, as before, the system weakened and disintegrated with the coming of a new rational- ism and literalism.

57

38 Antonio Correggio. Cupola, c. 1526–30. Parma Cathedral

39 Andrea Pozzo. *Apotheosis of St Ignatius*, 1691–94. S. Ignazio, Rome >

40 Anton Raphael Mengs. *Parnassus*, 1761. Villa Albani, Rome

The eighteenth-century Neoclassicists got tired of looking into heaven
and shunned this form of illusionism. A wall is a wall and a ceiling
a ceiling. The *Parnassus* by Anton Raphael Mengs in the Villa Albani
in Rome passes as one of the first symptoms of this attitude. You could
not tell from the illustration that it was a ceiling painting and not a
mural. In Neoclassicism the decorative picture became increasingly
subservient to the aim of lucid organization, as exemplified in the
Etruscan Room designed by Robert Adam for Osterley.

Lecturing to the students of the Royal Academy at the turn of the
century, Henry Fuseli came to speak of the lost murals by Polygnotus
in Delphi which I mentioned at the beginning of this lecture and which,
by that time, had become the subject of much debate among classical
scholars and artists, who attempted to reconstruct their appearance on

60

41 Robert Adam. Etruscan Room, 1775–77. Osterley House, London >

42 Pierre Puvis de Chavannes. *The Sciences and the Arts*, 1887.

the basis of the description by Pausanias. Remember that Goethe's diagram of the arrangement (p. 19) shows the more remote figures higher up on the wall. Taking note of this compositional principle, Fuseli warned his hearers not 'to impute solely to ignorance or imbecility what might rest on the firm base of permanent principle':

At that summit, art shuns the rules prescribed to inferior excellence and . . . returns to its elements. . . . Simplicity, parallelism, apposition, take place of variety, contrast and composition. . . . We must incline to ascribe the primitive arrangement of the whole rather to the artist's choice and lofty simplicity than want of comprehension.[28]

In the course of the nineteenth century this preference for primitive methods of composition over illusionism in decorative painting was

Grand Amphithéâtre, Sorbonne, Paris

destined to become an article of faith among the reformers of design.
Pugin emulated the tact of medieval designers, who avoided the pit-
falls of illusionistic motifs; he specifically mentioned that wallpapers
should never show shadowed objects, because their painted shadow,
when repeated all round the room, would come into conflict with the
real shadows cast by the light from the windows.[29] Maybe the literal-
minded Victorians underrated the capacity of the human mind to
take fiction as fiction.

When, in 1852, the zealous reformer Sir Henry Cole arranged an
exhibition at Marlborough House of visual atrocities which the
cultivated designer should learn to shun, he did not fail to include
paper hangings which are severely criticized in the official catalogue
for showing 'natural objects in unseemly position, horses and ground

43 Ferdinand Hodler. *The Retreat from Marignano*, 1896–1900.

floating in the air, objects much out of scale'.[30] Shades of Leonardo!

In the inevitable conflict between the means of illusion and the ends of decorative design, illusion was rapidly losing its hold on the visual image. The decorators were in the van of those who decried the vulgarity of illusionistic tricks, and the leading masters of the mural came to adopt their dogma. Pierre Puvis de Chavannes said that if an

Schweizerisches Landesmuseum, Zürich

artist failed to respect the wall, the wall would reject his work. The expression he used was more drastic, and is better left untranslated.[31] From Puvis the message was taken up by Ferdinand Hodler in Switzerland, who championed as the true principle of art the idea of 'parallelism' [32] – the very term Fuseli had used in his description of the lost murals by Polygnotus. But even Hodler's monumental murals were

65

too robust for the next generation of Art Nouveau, who much admired them but who had discovered in the East and in Byzantine art new sources of inspiration – witness Gustav Klimt's mosaic decoration of the dining-room of the Palais Stoclet in Brussels, with its near-abstract play of flat shapes.

These designs date from 1905–09, and by this time the crisis which disrupted Leonardo's unities in mural decoration had also spread to easel painting. But that, you will be relieved to hear me say, is a different story.

44 Gustav Klimt. Mosaic frieze, 1909–11. Dining-room, Palais Stoclet, Brussels

NOTES

LIST AND SOURCES OF ILLUSTRATIONS

NOTES

1 New York and London 1960. See also my Romanes Lecture, *Art History and The Social Sciences*, Oxford 1975.

2 *Gesammelte Schriften*, Berlin 1932, pp. 95–158.

3 Leonardo da Vinci, *Treatise on Painting*, ed. A. Philip McMahon, Princeton, N.J., 1956, No. 265 (Cod. Urb. 47 r & v). Translations in the text are mine.

4 Ed. cit., No. 418 (Cod. Urb. 108).

5 London 1960.

6 Ed. cit., No. 265 (Cod. Urb. 47 v).

7 Ed. cit., No. 267 (Cod. Urb. 61 r).

8 Emanuel Löwy, *Polygnot*, Vienna 1929.

9 Pausanias, Book X, 25–31.

10 J. W. von Goethe, *Über Polygnots Gemälde in der Lesche zu Delphi*, 1803.

11 E. Pfuhl, *Malerei und Zeichnung der Griechen*, Munich 1923.

12 Vitruvius, *On Architecture*, Book 7, 5.

13 See my *Norm and Form*, London 1966, pp. 83 ff.

14 Giacomo Grimaldi, *Descrizione della Basilica di S. Pietro in Vaticano*, ed. Reto Niggl, Vatican City 1972; see also J. Garber, *Wirkungen der frühchristlichen Gemäldezyklen der alten Peters und Pauls Basilika in Rom*, Berlin–Vienna 1918.

15 I am referring to the seated woman in the scene of the Adoration of the Magi who has been interpreted as Ecclesia or as Divine Wisdom.

16 O. Demus, *Romanesque Mural Painting*, London and New York 1970.

17 *L'art religieux de la fin du Moyen-Age en France*, Paris 1908.

18 *The Mirrour of the Blessed Lyfe of Jesu Christ*, ed. Lawrence F. Powell, Oxford 1908.

19 See my 'Action and Expression in Western Art', in *Non-Verbal Communication*, ed. R. A. Hinde, Cambridge 1972, and 'The Leaven of Criticism in Renaissance Art', in *The Heritage of Apelles*, London 1976.

20 See my *Symbolic Images*, London 1972, pp. 15–16.

21 Upsala 1963; for the status of personifications see my *Symbolic Images* cited above.

22 L.B. Alberti, *On Painting*, ed. C Grayson, London 1972, p. 49.

23 Dr Kim Veltman has kindly drawn my attention to a note by Leonardo in the Codex Atlanticus, 111 v.b. which indicates that Leonardo was aware of the fact that figures in paintings appear to shift as the observer moves.

24 *Francesco Salviati au Palais Sacchetti de Rome et la décoration murale italienne (1520–1560)*, Geneva 1973, which also contains a full bibliography.

25 See my Romanes lecture cited above (note 1).

26 A. Blunt, 'Illusionist Decoration in Central Italian Painting of the Renaissance', in *Journal of the Royal Society of Arts*, April 1959.

27 See my Icones Symbolicae in *Symbolic Images*, especially pp. 153–6.

28 *Lectures on Painting by the Royal Academicians*, ed. R.N. Wornum, London 1889, p. 355. The famous antiquarian the Comte de Caylus had published a 'Description de deux tableaux de Polygnote donnée par Pausanias' in the *Histoire de l'Académie Royale des Inscriptions et Belles Lettres*, 27, 1761, pp. 34–55, for which Le Lorrain had provided pictorial illustrations. These had given E. Falconet, in his translation of Pliny (*Traduction du xxxiv, xxxv, et xxxvi livres de Pline l'Ancien* . . . , 2nd edn., The Hague 1773, I, 248), another opportunity of venting his spite on the ancients he considered much overrated. I am indebted for this explanation of Fuseli's remark to Mr Alex Potts.

29 A. Bøe, *From Gothic Revival to Functional Form*, Oslo 1957.

30 *Department of Practical Art: Catalogue of the Articles of Ornamental Art*, London 1852, Appendix No. 23.

31 'S'il se f . . . de la muraille . . . la muraille le vomira', M. Vachon, *Puvis de Chavannes*, Paris 1895, p. 115.

32 His lecture 'Die Sendung des Künstlers' is reprinted in *Die Krise der Kunst*, ed. S. Rudolph, Stuttgart 1948.

LIST AND SOURCES OF ILLUSTRATIONS

72